AF244622

Written by
JESSICA OGUEKWE

Written during the NaNoWriMo
Young Writers Program

NaNoWriMo 2018 event.

If you are a parent reading this book,
I want you to read it with an open mind
because this book will help you know
what your child really wants from you.

If you know already, it will remind you
again.

TABLE OF CONTENT

Chapter 6: Every child wants their birthday to be remembered and celebrated as much as possible.

Chapter 7: Every child wants to know that their parents love them, they wants to feel important.

Interview

Conclusion

INTRODUCTION

My name is Jessica Oguekwe; I am 12 years, blessed with a Mum, Dad and 2 brothers, Roniel and Aviel.

What I'm about to write in this book is my experience as a child in a family, and I have lovely parents.

If you are a parent reading this book I want you to read it with an open mind, because this book will help you know what your child/ children really wants from you, if you know already, it will remind you again.

I know every parent's desire is to give their children the best of life and make them happy, but the truth is sometimes, we give them what we think they like, which might not be what they really want from their parent at a given time and they might not have the guts to speak out.

I acknowledge that the primary concern of every parent is to provide the basic needs, which are; food, shelter, education.... The list goes on. But there are other needs which I believe this book will highlight.

This book is loaded with my experience, my friends' and other children through interview I had with them; children from 10 years to 17 years of age. Hopefully you will learn some truths from this book and know a better way of meeting the needs of your children.

Meeting our needs is more important than giving us gifts.

DEDICATION

I would like to dedicate this book to God the giver of life, the **CREATOR** of the world because without God none of this would be possible so all the Glory goes to Him.

And to you my readers, thanks for reading.

ACKNOWLEDGMENT

I would like to appreciate some of the people that helped me with this book

God for the inspiration, opportunity and the help to create this book.

My mom and dad for giving me the support to write this book.

Special thanks to my Dad for editing and proofreading.

Rev. Funke Adetubero for giving me the Topic and Platform to speak in one of her program in IRELAND, Ma I'm grateful.

FOREWORD

CHILDREN ARE A SPECIAL GIFT FROM GOD

Children are a special gift from God. It says in psalms 127: 3-5

"Lo, children are an heritage from the Lord: and the fruit of the womb is his reward. As arrows are in the hand of a mighty man; so are the children of the youth. Happy is the man that hath his quiver full of them: they shall not be ashamed, but shall speak with the enemies in the gate" (KJV).

As you can see in the bible verse, having a child is a special thing and we should not take it for granted. Every parent is a worthy Steward, which is why God gave you those child/children, so try your best to understand, know and meet their needs.

Taking from REV. FUNKE ADETUBERU's teaching on a CD I listened to, "when a baby is born they have their fists clutched and they look up to their mother and say "are you worthy of being my parent, will you take care of me the best you can, will you help me grow up to be the person I am meant to be?". These questions are still in our hearts.

Children are very special and deserve to be taken care of properly. Therefore, I believe this book will help you recognize

some of the things your child/children need from you, that will help them grow and come to trust you more, so that when they ever need help or advice they can easily come to you, because they know you understand and desire the best for them.

CHAPTER 1

WE NEED OUR PARENTS TO LISTEN TO US

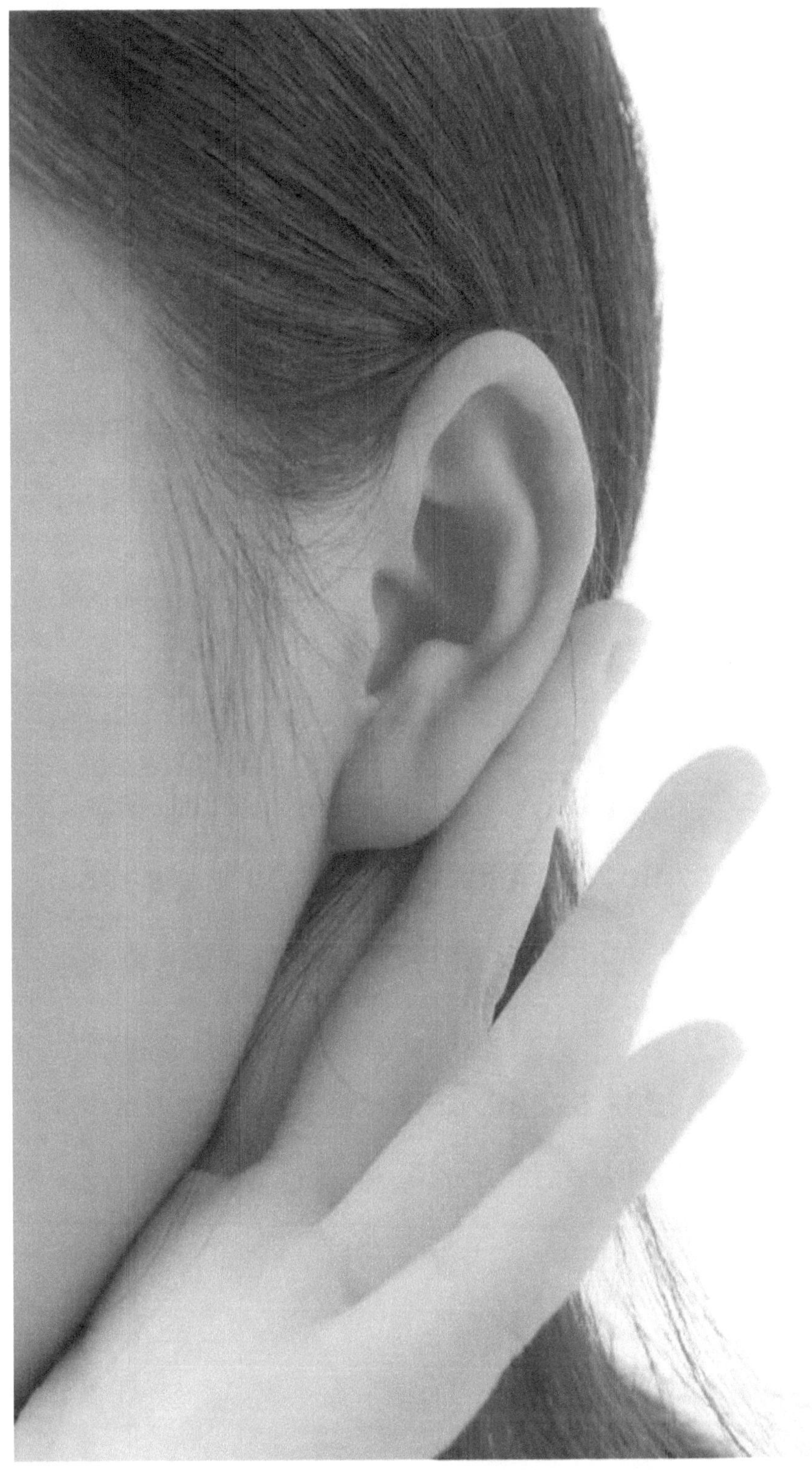

"To listen is to give attention to sound or action, when listening, one is hearing what others are saying, and trying to understand what it means. The act of listening involves complex affective, cognitive, and behavioral processes" (Oxford Living Dictionaries).

Listening is a very important skill, and a basic requirement in parent and child relationship, but most of our parents have not really harness this skill. Everyone has the ability to listen, at least I hope, but sometimes it seems as if our parent do not want or do not believe we should be listened to.

There are acts by parents that indicate a child is not been listened to. Some of them are as follow:

1. Impatient:

Impatience is simply lack of patience and easily provoked. It is also the feeling of being irritated by someone's mistake, or annoyed, not wanting to wait, expecting something to happen quickly.

This usually occur when a child makes a mistake or do something wrong that gets their parents angry.

In most cases, opportunity is not given to the child to explain, because the parents are too upset to listen. The ability to listen to your child even when you are annoyed with them is priceless, and one of the greatest need of a child. Sometimes, parent's impatience are based on expectation placed on their child/children, which might not be met as they expected. There is no doubt in my heart that all parents love their children, but please listen to us irrespective of the outcome of our action or the childishness that is part of our growing up.

2. Too Busy

In this time and age, most of our parents are working, schooling, raising family, involved in community activities, trying to make sure everything is in order; we have enough to eat, house to live in, all bills are paid, and children education is taken care of etc., all these are great, but trying to get all things under control, sometimes affect parents ability to attend to their children at the end of the day. The truth is that they are exhausted with all the day's activities; however, the ability to listen to your child even in the mist of your busy schedules is a great skill.

In my experience, sometimes when my mum is busy cooking or on her phone, my younger brother would come to her and say, "mum can I have this?" my mum without looking at what he is asking for will say okay you can have it. But when she is done with whatever she was doing when my brother made the request, then her attention is drawn to what has been taken from the table, as if there was never a communication, that is when my brother will say, "but mum you said I can have it", and my mum will say, "when did I say that?". Can you see what happened here? My mum was so busy and didn't pay full attention to what my younger brother was asking for.

Does this sound familiar? This happens most times with mummies and daddies; if not dealt with, could actually lead to something more serious that could hurt your child. Please always pay full attention when your child/children communicates, no matter what you are doing, I tell you the truth, everything can wait, nothing is more important than your child's life.

3. You can predict what your child wants to say.

This is an assumption most parents tend to have, and it often lead to them not waiting for us to finish a statement before cutting

in. this happens because our parents believe they know us so well, and they know what we are about to say before we say it, but that's not true most of the time. Every child has their own mind and their voice and should be allowed to speak and to be listened to. Some times when I want to say some things to my parents, they sometimes say "Jessica I know what you want to say, that's okay now, please go back to your room", or they will say Jessica, "I know what you want to say, we will talk about it later". The truth is that as much as my parents know me or believe they can predict me, it does not guarantee that they know what I wanted to say, but what can I

do? I am the child and they are the parents who love me so much. In such case, I will quietly go back to my room, and I might not remember what I wanted to tell them.

I believe it is proper to hear your child out every time, even when they don't make sense, because they might have an important message to pass, and if not given the opportunity to say it, this might lead them to making wrong decisions or they might fall into wrong hands trying to get answers to their questions. Please Daddies and Mummies always listen to your child/children, this singular act can save

their soul from destruction, and from
outside influence.

CHAPTER 2

UNDERSTAND AND KNOW US

"To understand is to know the meaning of something that someone says: to know how someone feels or why someone behave in a particular way" (Cambridge English Dictionary).

Understanding and knowing your child/children is crucial in a family relationship. In order to know your child/children you have to make effort and take out time to stay with them, allow them do most of the talking when you are with them, and be part of their lives (daily activities if possible). Do you really want to understand and know your Child/children? Then practice the following:

Spend time with your child:

When you spend time with your child/children, you will get to discover some things you never knew about them. Spending time with your child/children is a need in the life of children especially when they are younger, and a requirement for proper development. When parents understand their children at early stage, it helps to guide them as they grow. The inability of most parents to know and understand their child/children has led to mistaken assumptions about their child/children, and as you and I will agree, every assumption not proven is wrong.

Although I'm not a teenager yet, but I have come to notice that when most children get to teenage age, they don't really want to spend time with their parents any more, they prefer to stay with friends, at least I have a lot of teenagers around me so, I might be right. My elder brother for example, who is in his teenage years, prefers to stay in his room chatting with his friends than coming down stairs to the dinning or sitting area to spend time with the family. So parents enjoy it while it last, before we all become teenagers and you find yourself sitting alone.

In my experience, spending time with your child/children is really good, I enjoy spending time with my parents, it is fun for me, at times I don't want my mum to go to work, all because I just want to stay around her, and when my dad goes out to do some things, I will keep asking my mum when is my dad coming back, I can ask this question a hundred times, I always like to initiate family time together in my home; eating dinner together, playing games, watching movies, at times it works out well, but some of the time, if not most, my teenage brother wants to go to his room and stay on his own or chat with friends on his phone, except when there is a basketball game on, which I painfully join to watch, just to have family time.

I do believe that, if our parents spends time with us at our younger age, it will help them to understand and know us better as we grow older.

Allow your child to talk:
Do you really want to understand and know your child? Then you have to allow them to do the talking when spending time with them. Let them tell you their stories, how their day went, about their friends, their teachers, anything they want to talk about, in doing so you will know and understand

how they reason, how they see life, their social skills, and how they behave in school.

For example I enjoy telling my parents how my day went, what happened in school or how I dealt with situation that went on in the course of my day, I noticed that some of the time my parents correct me in some of the situations where I dealt with issues in the wrong way. This happened because they allowed me do most of the talking. I have come to know that when young people are allowed to talk they tend to sell their secrets without knowing. Please daddies and mummies allow your children to do most of the talking when you spend time with them, this will help you to understand and know them better.

Be part of their lives:

To get to know and understand us better you need to be part of our live, i.e. our daily activities, sports, school, church, our dreams etc. in doing these you will learn what we like, how we react to things, how we deal with things or why we do things. By this practices you will also build a stronger connection with your child/ children. For example, I'm always over excited when I'm having a school play, or any school functions and one or both of my parents are able to attend, and watch me perform, this boost

my confidence, it makes me feel happy, feel loved and cherished. I can seriously affirm that my parents are so much involved in our lives, they do their best to be part of our lives.

My parents make sure they support us in our life chosen dreams, my brothers' plays basketball, my dad and mum takes them to all their training and matches no matter where it is, what day it fall into and the cost. They also support me so much in my own dreams as well. I give them 100% for this. Do you know that when you are involved in your child's life, you will be able to identify when they are going astray or

when they are being wrongly influenced by friends or their environment? Being part of our lives, is one of the great needs in our lives, we will really love you to meet as much as Possible.

Know your children's strengths:

When you know and understand your child, you are able to identify their strengths and know what areas they need improvements. There is always room for improvement in every child, but it requires parental understanding to identify them. You can assist them grow as a person by building their strengths and helping then reach their full potentials. Knowledge is power. Do all you can to know and understand your child.

One of the best and most obvious thing about Understanding and knowing your children is that it helps in developing stronger relationships with them, and it builds healthy family relationship and happy children. The benefits are endless, so set aside time to get to know and understand your child/children.

CHAPTER 3

WE NEED OUR PARENTS FOR GUIDANCE

"Guidance is to help and advice about how to do something or about how to deal with problems connected with your work, education, or personal relationship" (Cambridge English Dictionary).

Guidance is very essential in a growing child's life, children might not really think the need it that much, but it is very important in our lives, our parents has seen a lot of happenings, have experienced a lot, therefore, i know they are in the best position to guide us.

Guidance:

Guidance is an act of helping, giving assistance, advice, directions. Every child needs guidance from their parents especially at a young age, because if they are well guided at a younger age, it will have a positive effect in their lives as they grow. For example I know that every time I make mistake or do something wrong my parents will always make sure they sit me down and talk about what I did wrong, why it was wrong, and the right thing to do, so that I will not make the same mistake in the future. My parents also have a way of teaching me how to fix the wrong, instead of doing it for me. So that in the future, when I make mistake, I can right my wrong myself. I believe this is a good example of how to guide a child.

In letting your child right her wrong or fix her mistakes helps the child to practice problem solving skills. From most of my interview with peers, I discover that what some parents do, when their child/ children makes mistake, is to fix the problem by themselves, and not explaining to the child, what they've done wrong and how to go about fixing it. I am not sure why this is the case, but if it does happen, parent please trust that children can learn

if properly taught. Therefore, the best way is to take them through the process, not just doing it for them. Doing it for them is just like when a teacher gives out a test and writes down all the answers without giving the child the chance to think for themselves.

Every child needs opportunities to practice their Problem solving skills, all we need from our parents is to guide us, direct us, but don't be us, psalms 139 verse 48 part A says **"we are fearfully and wonderfully made by God"** which means that God made everyone to be amazing before he released us, He put in us the potential and capability

to do great things, to be initiative. Dear mum and dad, guide us but allow us to use our initiative.

THINGS YOU CAN DO TO HELP GUIDE YOUR CHILD

1. EXPLAIN RULES IN ADVANCE:

Your children need to know what they are allowed to do and what they are not allowed to do, set limits, let them know what happens when they do what is not allowed. Truthfully how is anyone supposed to know what to do if they are not told? Parents

need to be firm when explaining to their children the rules and the set limits. If you want them to follow these rules, they need to know the consequences of breaking them. For example, if your child starts bullying another child, or make fun of them, and call them names, you as a parents needs to show them that it is wrong, and make them apologies. The consequence could be no dessert for 4 days.

If they continually stay pass their bedtime, they might need to go to bed an hour earlier for a week, as a way of teaching them not to break set down rules.

If they turn on the television first thing on a weekend morning, this will result to no television for the rest of the day, this is one of the way my mum deals with my younger brother's attitude of breaking the "no TV on weekend morning till noon rule in our house".

In our house, you are not allowed to put on television on school days, unless our parents turns it on in the evenings, however, on weekends or holidays we are allowed to put on TV from 12 noon. But it's been very hard for my younger brother to keep to this particular rule in the house, so some Saturdays, he will come down early

when everyone is still in bed and turn on the TV, when my mum comes down and see him on the TV or I tell on him, my mum will stop him from watching TV for one or two weeks. This method seems to be working in our home. Now what my younger brother does is to keep his eyes on the clock, when it is 12 on the dot, he goes for the TV remote as if his life depends on it. (Is that not funny?)

Most times when my parents set rules in the house, I try my best to keep them, not that I'm the perfect one, but I do really try my best to keep to rules. I have noticed that sometimes when my brothers break the rules and I tell on them, my mum will either let them face the consequences of breaking the rules, or just say Jessica don't worry I will look into it, and when she says that, I know that she wants to give them a pass this time, which is actually a mother's heart. But I also believe that, when a child finds out that they can go free from breaking rules, they will keep breaking bigger rules even outside of their home (This is just my thinking, I might be wrong remember I'm just a child).

Your children need to know the rules, to follow them and they need to know that there are consequences for not keeping to the rules.

2. INVOLVE YOUR CHILDREN IN SETTING FAMILY RULES:

Children tend to pay more attention to or think highly of things they are involved in. So if your child/children help set the rules at home or are involved in the process, they might start to think that having and keeping to rules is very important. Knowing they are part of setting the rules, places an obligation on them not to break it.

3. ENCOURAGE GOOD BEHAVIOR WITH REWARDS:

Children love rewards and if they know that the better they act the more rewards they get, they will start behaving well, because they know that they get rewarded for good works. Good behavior reward system in homes helps character building in children, and continuous practice of this pattern can develop into a life style. This system guarantees good mannered and well behaved child.

For example: When your child finish tidying up their room you can say "good job, now we can go out for pizza"

Or your child finishes their homework you can say "good work, now let's play that board game of yours"

In our home, when I clean my room and the kitchen I get 50cents into my savings, both of my brothers get rewarded as well for doing some chores, we take it seriously because of the reward system in place. We are saving towards our summer holiday, so we all are willing to do all our chores to earn that money, now cleaning up the house is becoming a lifestyle for us.

Please parents remember this reward system works in our home, you don't have to use it. Check for what will work in your own home, but do your best to add a system that reward good deeds.

4. SPEAK POSITIVE:

Children take it in better when they are corrected positively, than been spoken to negatively because of a mistake. For example:

Instead of saying "you made a big mess, now go tidy up your room " say " darling your

room is a bit messy could you go and tidy it up please "

Instead of "get away from that glass " say " sweetie that glass is very fragile, come beside me so it will not break "

5. IRON IT OUT:

Children make mistakes and might not even know they did, but in this situation the best thing to do, is to sit your child down, tell them what they did wrong, show them how to fix it and if it was a genuine mistake let them know that they are forgiven.

6. TEACH BY EXAMPLE:

Modeling good behavior to a child is another great need in a child's life. Children most time mirror the behavior of the people they spend the most time with, if they are not learning the best behavior from you, then who are they learning it from? Every GIRL wants to be like their mum and every boy wants to be like their dad, they believe that their parents are the best example of what a person should be, and often their greatest model, so please parents do what you say, because children learn by examples. If you want your children to be clean, please do keep a clean environment, not only saying, please clean your room, or the house, the child wants to see you clean, so that they can learn from you.

I learnt this from my dad, he cleans our rooms for us and then makes us follow the example he has set in cleaning the rooms. That is teaching by example, he always wants us to see what he is doing and learn from that, my mum is a little different from my dad, my mum wants you to learn on the job, she will be doing it with you and the next time, she will watch you do it, and another time, she will ask you to do it on your own, which is still another good way of modelling for your child to see. In our house we watch our parents, Pray, read their bibles, fast and being nice to people. What I'm trying to say here is that it is very good to be a good Model to your child, we learn faster by what we see you do, not what you say. BE A GOOD ROLE MODEL. Every parent want their children/child to be great, but you know as the saying goes "the apple does not fall far from its tree", children learn faster from example, if you want your child/children to be honest, kind and decent to people, then you have to be honest, kind and decent, check yourself, are you the kind of person your children can look up to, look into your faults and your strengths, are you their perfect role model?

Please daddies and mummies guide us, but give us room so we will not be dormant and depend on you for everything.

CHAPTER 4

WE NEED OUR PARENTS TO TRUST AND HAVE FAITH IN US

"Trust is to believe that someone is good and honest and will not harm you, or that something is safe and reliable" (Cambridge English Dictionary)

Every child wants to know that they have the trust of their parents. We just want them to believe we are good and that we can represent them well. We want them to trust our dreams and the things we want to do in life.

Sometimes our parents think that they know what we want to be in the future, like my mom she wants me to be a medical doctor, but for now I just want to be

writer, actor, dancer, singer, model, I think I'm supposed to be in front of the camera, that's what I want to do, well that is a story for another day. Some of the time our parents feel like we should be what they want us to be in the future. It is not only about making your parents happy it is about being happy too.

Why?

Because when you do not trust your child it does not only make us afraid to go into the world and experience new things, but it also slowly breaks the bond between a child and their parents. A healthy relationship

between a parent and their child is a very important thing to keep and to do that, you have to fully trust them and they have to trust you.

Our parents want us to trust them with everything they do, but when we try and do something ourselves it appears to be wrong, we know you want us to be safe, but covering us from the world is equally destructive.

However, I still think children need to earn that trust, they have to keep good grades in school, be polite, clean the house.

Overall what I am saying is when you give respect, you get respect, when you trust, you get trust. **Just give and it will come back to you, what goes around comes around.** So parents if you trust your children, you will also earn their trust.

Dear parents trust us, have faith in us, we will not disappoint you.

CHAPTER 5

EVERY CHILD WANTS TO BE CORRECTED WITH LOVE AND NOT WITH A SHOUT

"Correction is a change made to something in order to correct or improve it, or the action of making such a change" (Cambridge English Dictionary)

Every child makes mistakes at one point or the other, making mistake is part of growing up, parents also makes mistakes sometimes, that means everyone makes mistakes sometimes. Most times when we as children make mistakes, it really is a genuine mistake, which we want to learn from, and not be scared of it. We love our parents so much we just want to know you love us too, yes sometimes the love approach does not work and some children will soon think they can get away with anything. I know sometimes some parents shout at their child/children, I know it is out of love they are doing it, but if you keep shouting at your child, they will be scared to make mistake and this lead to the child been timid, and not wanting to try things for the fear of making mistake.

I carried out a research on the effects of shouting on children, which I will discuss in a moment, but first, I will like to state that no child is perfect, as a child I know sometimes we can push our parents to the extent where they do not even know that

they are shouting and sometimes we children do not even know when we are talking back. Countless acts by children are the reason for this shouting; not doing our chores or start fight with our brothers and sisters and these things can make the most calm parent start shouting and sometimes children react by talking back or not do there chores to make a point or a statement. Yes there are better ways to do things, but because we are still growing and learning we might not do things correctly. With my young experience I found out some of the reasons why parents yell.

Parents yell out of pure frustration, and not because they dislike their children, because no parent hates their child. No child also wants to leave their everyday life having their parent shouting at them. Shouting at your child does not solve the problem it might keep them quiet and obedient for a while, but it will not fix their behavior or attitude problems, all it does is make them scared of you.

According to Laura Markham who is an author and parent educator, "your number one job as a parent, after assuring the safety and health of your children is to manage your own emotions". Therefore, if

our parents can control their emotions in every giving situation with regards to our mistake, they will be able to correct us with love.

Research has shown that long term exposure to shouting can result in low self-esteem, fear, anxiety, insomnia, lack of confident in what a person can do, academic problems, difficulties in their social life, emotional instability, thwarted coping skills and behavior problems.

Dear parents, sometimes it is better you allow us to make the mistake and learn from

it, and do correct us in love and not always with a shout or punishment.

My prayer is that God will give every parent the wisdom on how to correct their child/children; I know parenting is NOT easy, sometimes I look at my mom, I feel her frustration on when she is trying to correct us and it looks as if we don't get it, at times I do ask her, "Mom how are you coping with some of our behaviors especially with my brothers" because I don't really give her problems. In as much as I have said this, I still want every parent to know that every child is different and

unique, and understands things in different ways.

Dads and mummies, when we make mistake forgive us and let us know that you have forgiven us, so we can move forward.

CHAPTER 6

EVERY CHILD WANTS
THEIR BIRTHDAY TO
BE REMEMBERED AND
CELEBRATED AS MUCH
AS POSSIBLE

Most children love their birthdays to be remembered and celebrated, they want it to be one of the best days of their lives, but they also want to know that people, mostly close family members care about their birthday, which is the day they were born. I remembered my mum telling me, that when she was younger her parents do celebrate all of their birthdays (hers and her sibling), because their parents understood that it was a special day to be celebrated.

It does not matter how small or big it was, the important thing is that it is been done, and they all enjoyed and were very happy.

I remember on my eleventh birthday there was heavy snow in Ireland on that day, so we could not go out to celebrate, which normally is the custom in our house. We always celebrate everyone's birthday, no matter how small, so on that snowy day because we could not go out, we decided to do something in-house.

That special day which was my birthday, we baked a cake and did as much as we could do to celebrate my birthday and it was one of the best day ever. What I am saying is that, children enjoy it when a day is brought out specially to celebrate them,

they feel loved, cherished and over excited.

Dear daddies and mummies, please do your best to celebrate all your children's birthdays no matter how old or young they are, they need to be celebrated in your own little way, it must not be big, if you cannot afford it big, it could be small but special. Because they deserve it.

CHAPTER 7

EVERY CHILD WANTS
TO KNOW THAT THEIR
PARENTS LOVE THEM,
THEY WANTS TO FEEL
IMPORTANT,

Being loved is part of children's needs, every child wants to know that their parent love them, I know you will say if you don't love us, why will you give us food, shelter, education etc., that sounds like my parents! We know you do all these, but we still want to hear you say **'I love you'**, children wants to hear that from their parents, it is so **reassuring**. We know you act it, but we want to **hear** it.

Feeling important, comes from being loved, make me feel special, do not compare me to anyone, no matter who, not even my siblings, you can motivate me with good

things people are doing, but not in comparison.

I am me, I am special, I am me, I am unique, I am me, I am specially and wonderfully made by God, please let me feel important. Tell me you are doing great, but you can do better, tell me I am very smart, let me know i am beautiful, tell me I am well behaved. Look for good words and tell me, help me always see the positive side of me, and let me know that there is room to improve on my weakness.

Do you know the truth? When you make your child feel love and important, when they go out to the really world, they will not be **intimidated** by anyone, who wants to **bully** them or who want to bring them down. Because their confidence and self-esteem has been built from home, they can stand any oppression anyone tries to throw at them. Mummies and daddies make us **feel loved and important.**

Every child wants to feel important, to know that their parents love them, and it will make your child's day, that once in a while you tell them, **'you're doing well thank you'**, it should not matter how much they have done, just try and always appreciate them, because from there they can learn how to appreciate even little acts of kindness in people. Everyone has to know they are not taken for granted and your child want to know that they are not taken for granted. Truth be told, "who does not want to be appreciated???"

INTERVIEW WITH MY FRIENDS

Jessica: My first question is: What do you need from both of your parents?

Friends: We need their love, kindness, and understanding.

Jessica: And from your mother?

Friends: We need her guidance. We want to be able to talk to her without judgment and we need her to listen.

Jessica: And from your father?

Friends: We need him to trust our decisions and listen to us.

Jessica: How do you feel when your parents do not listen to you?

Friends: We feel irrelevant, sad and disappointed because we listen to them but they do not listen to us.

Jessica: What is the next step you take when your parents do not listen to you?

Friends: Well, we try to keep our emotions under control as much as we can so we do not get into trouble.

Generally we try to keep calm and let out our anger quietly.

Jessica: Thank you very much.

Jessica: In conclusion, with the help of my friends this is what I found out. Most children need their parents to listen, guide, love, and understand them.

A happy child is a happy home.

CONCLUSION

Now you have reached the end of this book, and I hoped it has helped. The purpose of this book is to bring to parents' attention some of the things their children need from them, which they might already know or have taken for granted. To ensure parents and children bonding, this is the hallmark of a happy home.

AND REMEMBER IT IS ALL ABOUT JESUS, SHARE, COMMENT, LEARN AND HAVE A Happy Home!!!

9 781916 125612